Words Lost in the Brain
Copyright © 2024 LaDonna Akens Elam

Produced and printed by Stillwater River Publications.
All rights reserved. Written and produced in the United States of America.
This book may not be reproduced or sold in any form without the expressed, written permission of the author(s) and publisher.

Visit our website at **www.StillwaterPress.com** for more information.

First Stillwater River Publications Edition

ISBN: 978-1-960505-63-7

Library of Congress Control Number: 2023915598

1 2 3 4 5 6 7 8 9 10

Written by LaDonna Akens Elam.
Cover and interior design by Elisha Gillette.
Published by Stillwater River Publications,
West Warwick, RI, USA.

*The views and opinions expressed
in this book are solely those of the author(s)
and do not necessarily reflect the views
and opinions of the publisher.*

The earliest poems remain the same as I wrote them down to see how aphasia works through me. Occasionally words will have an asterisk (*) by them. Another word will be printed at the bottom to explain the author's intent. If a word was left out, asterisks (*) will also be used to clarify meaning.

Words Lost in the Brain

ACKNOWLEDGEMENTS

Jesus

Family

Sunrise

First Therapy to STAR: Dr. Corwin, Samye, Carolyn, Mellissa, SLP's

Poem in Speech-Mark Harder and Poetry Friends

I would like to acknowledge many people who have been with me through my stroke and aphasia. I pray I don't miss anyone but if I have, please know I remember you in my heart. The first and foremost is Dr. Melinda Corwin, Ph.D., CCC-SLP, she has been with me for the entire 6 plus years since my stroke. She has provided me with care and kindness along with stroke recovery, camp, and teaching me to keep moving forward. Samye Hildebrandt, M.S., CCC-SLP, Carolyn Perry, M.S., CCC-SLP, Mellissa Whitaker, M.S., CCC-SLP, and Dr. Dembowski, Ph.D., CCC-SLP, retired, have all been with the STroke Aphasia Recovery Program (STAR), for the 6 1/2 years I have been here. They are all wonderful people and have helped me relearn speech, numbers, words, writing, reading, music, art and theatre through therapy and camp. Each one has been a part of my book that I have been writing. I am thankful to every one of them.

My family have been some wonderful people to help me get through my stroke and aphasia every day. My husband, Kevin, has been beside me all the way pushing me and being present. My son, Scotty, is my caregiver at STAR. He is a wonderful person and has taken care of

everyone. My daughters, Kim and Shawna, call me quite often, which really means the world to me and reminds me that I'm important! My dad, Donald Akens, would call me every evening when I first had my stroke to check on me. Now he calls me every week and I am just so thankful for that, to continue to have my dad.

Now much of my time is spent with friends on Facebook, through ARC (Aphasia Recovery Connection), and Poems and Speech with Mark Harder. Many of these people have taught me so many things, listened to my poems, and have given me the opportunity to listen to theirs. If you ever have a chance to check them out, many of them have their own books, they are fantastic!

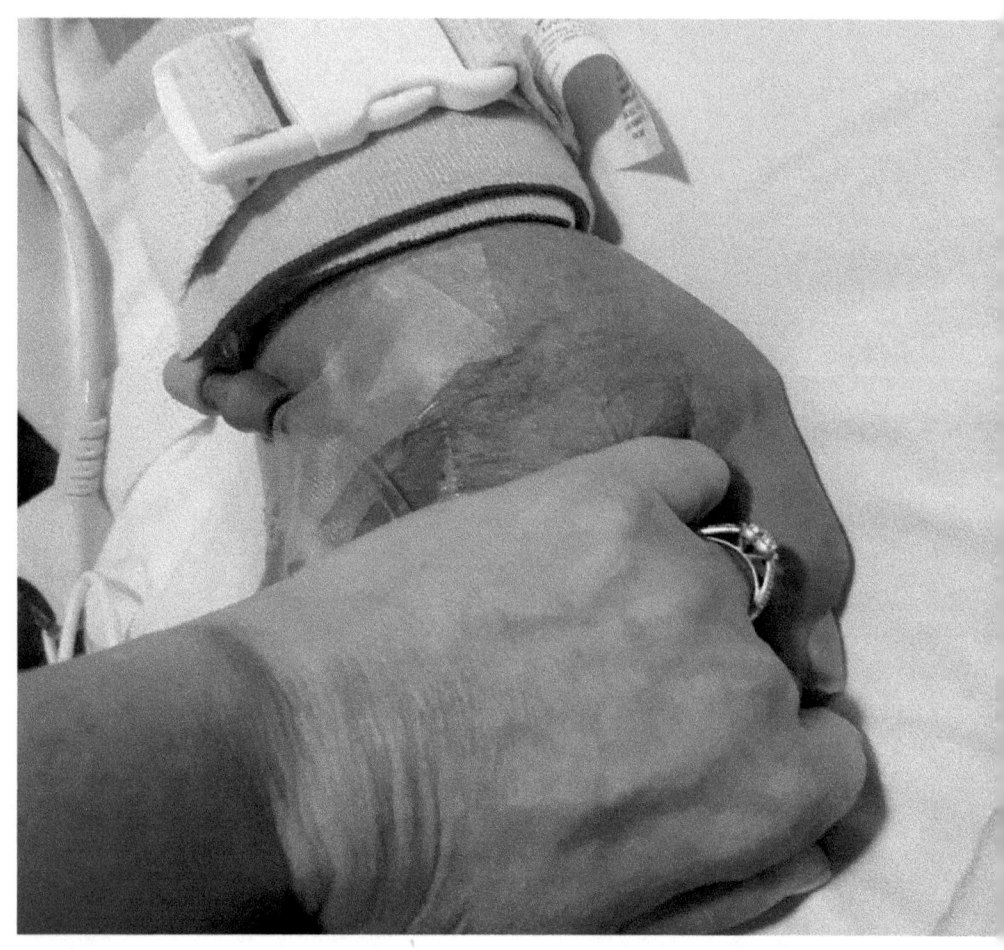

*This is a picture from the day I had my stroke.
My daughter, Kim, is holding my hand.*

1 The Person I Used to Be
4/12/18

I went to sleep for a few days
I woke up and I couldn't remember
anybody
I had many Test
Trying to figure out how to eat
Seeing if I can even figure out how to go
to the bathroom
I remember faces that I'm supposed
to know
The man who took care of me every day
and treated me like a queen
My wonderful kids and grandkids came to
see me even if I didn't know who they were
Friends came talk to me and tell me I
was looking good
They tell me everything was good enough
now to go home
I try to get better every day
But I know that I will never be the person
I used to be
You see I had a stroke and will have a
Aphasia forever —

2 SCHEDULE—To Be or Not to Be
4/23/18

I need to have a schedule
For one I make to figure out what I
need every day
Like a person needs to make breakfast
And do dishes and laundry and dust
But I need to vacuum the floor and
clean the toilet to
And I would like to eater* the yard and do
some walking sometime to
The flowers grow and get the bird seeds
and watch what they do
Then somewhere I would like email
and play Facebook
And really spend time with my Bible
And spend a lot of time with my grandkids
you something funny

But most of the time I am what I call fluffy.
Fluffy is I get tired very easily.
And the brain just quits.
So most of the time I get to do one thing
Then the rest the day I have to rest.
So I don't know how to make a schedule
When it seems we will never have enough
time to do all these things
Because every day I'm just fluffy
And I can't do it by myself anymore
That's just the way it is every day.—

---

*   mow

3   But I'm just so tired already
         4/30/18

Take my medicine
I say goodbye for the day
I read a little email and Facebook
Time to put the clothes on
And do two loads of laundry
I need to take trash out
But I'm just so tired already
But I need to do the dishes
And I need to dust the room
The vacuum cleaner is dirty
But I'm just so tired already
I need to eater* the lawn
I need to walk a while
The dog would like to go
I need to go see my friends
But I'm just so tired already
There's so much that needs to be done
But I'm just so tired already —

---

*   mow

4   My Life is Different Now
5/30/18

I'm not whining
I'm not mad
I just want to explain
Explain that my life is different now

I can talk a lot
Takes me a while to while
figure out the right words
But it works OK most of the time

Reading is interesting
I have finally gotten
to where I can read most words
Don't always understand what they say

Writing is very different
Many times I can't figure out
how to write the words
It's very different and one thing that I
feel I really need

Math I have many problems
but I know that it will get better
Think I should understand i*
But sometimes I just can't figure it out

---

*   it

Understanding I have a difficult
time grasping
What comes into my brain many times
just doesn't make any sense
Many times I just have to say "I just
don't understand"

So I can only do one thing at a time
Take it slow and easy
and not worry I can't figure it out
It gets better and comes around

My body gets tired
And there's only so much I can do in a day
I try not to worry about the things
 I used to do
And I just pray that when I gets to
be too much

Sometimes other people may not
understand
And some may have their feelings hurt
because I'm different
I hope that I hear other people never
hurt each other
And that will always know that
God will take
care of everything —

5 God, Stroke, people change
7/17/18

Today, on July 17 2018
My stroke began 695 hours ago
There are many things that seem
to get better
But there are still many things that don't

I can now read words
But I can't understand what it says
I can't read* what others say much

I have learned to do repetitive things
But I cannot remember everything people
would like me to do
I can only do one thing at a time

I can do some housework
But it doesn't keep my house clean
I wear out too fast and can't get it all done

---

*   understand

I will have a stroke forever
I try not to be angry about it
I hope others would not ever be angry
at me either

I am thankful for God
Even though I can't always find out
my right words
God finds it in my heart to pray

I am thankful for everyone who
takes care me
I pray they know this every day
Be thankful for what you got —

6   Chasing Myself
9/13/18

I spend every day
Trying to remember
What my job was,
What chores that I make,*
What to do for my family,
Making gifts for my grandkids...
All those things
Are very important to me.
But now I am different,
With a stroke and aphasia.
Now trying to remember to
Studying** God,
Therapy, Reading and writing,
Remembering what to wear each day,
And some that I forget.
God reminds me I'm important.
I just hope that everyone else***
I still love everyone very much,
I just can't do everything I used to do. —

---

*   need to do
**   study
***   remembers

7   Aphasia is constantly searching
10/2/18

Cannot find the words I
want to say
Cannot write the words I
want to write
I cannot read the words I
want to read
Because I'm always
searching,
Trying to find the words
in my mind
And sometimes they are
just always searching.—

8   Stroke, what to do
10/29/17

There so much to do in a day.
I put my clothes on
Put* my medicine.
I put the dog out
Said goodbye to my husband.
I read my Bible
I listened to my Facebook friends for a bit.

Then I clean my birds,
The food, the poop and vacuum it all.
Five birds and watch in** dog,
Took me four hours to clean it all up.
But I think I did a great job!

My husband came home to eat his lunch,
It was nice for the visit and I love
him very much.
Afterward I finish vacuuming the rest
of the house,
And had to take up all the trash you
know it's stinks.
Then I had to mop the kitchen.

I am really crashing out today!
And I still need to do laundry
And make tea.
I'm already so tired!
I can't believe I used to do it all in
one day before,

But not today, just not today... —

---

*   take
**   the

9   how do you tell?
     11/1/18

I have had a stroke
I have aphasia
I can move my right side
But I can't feel it

Can't feel my hands
I get burnt sometimes accidentally
My legs have a tingle
that goes on a lot

I never know what might* "inside" feels like
hungry thirsty nauseated or more
Sometimes things** just "come out"
That's how it works these days

So when you think you might be ill
When you can't feel it
How do you tell someone?
How do you figure it out? —

---

*   my
**   words

10   God will provide
11/30/2018

I've been living for 59 years
I have four children
Many others others* that treat as my own
Which give me 26 grandchildren
And two great-grandchildren
All of whom I LOVE with all my heart

Used to give them all everything I had
They were everything to me every day
Thought it was my job
that if I can have it, it was there's**
as needed
I know it wasn't much but it was all I had

I still love them with all my heart
I just can't do it that way anymore
And I sure do hope that they understand
But life changes and I have to look***
That God will provide for all —

---

*   grandchildren
**   theirs
***   see

11   Sometimes I don't understand
12/15/18

It's been about two years
I've been doing OK
I can put my clothes on
I can clean house a little bit
And I can even make some dinner!

I don't get burned much anymore
And I don't fall anymore, which is great
I'm trying to get some exercise
Still can't drive
But I really think I'm doing great

But then for the last week
I feel that I can't understand things now
I'm dropping things more
Losing things more
And feeling like I can't figure it out

I don't know what causes this
But I know that it makes me sad
I know that I can't fix it
Don't know why it does it that way
Is it that way with a stroke every day? —

12   Dreams Can be Very Hard
1/15/19

I was going to work today
It was time for 341 meeting^{*}
I have to get the paperwork ready
And get me back to where I need to be

But then I couldn't find the paperwork
And I couldn't get back to where I
needed to be
And I couldn't tell people what I needed
I was just laying on the ground

I couldn't text
I couldn't call
I couldn't move
^{**}Just knew I was supposed to be
some where^{***}

Even in my dreams
I'm having another stroke
The Aphasia gets worse
And I can't get away —

---

*   my job's bankruptcy trustee meeting
**   I
***   a specific place that I can't remember

13   Why is it I can't remember?
         2/8/19

I can't always remember everything
*To take my medicine
That I need to get something
Just life stuff most of the time

But sometimes, just sometimes
Someone told me I Should** something
important
And I don't remember that***
But they tell you I told you

Could it be they have decided I didn't care?
I just chose not to?
I look away from**** what they said I needed?
And***** they never said it again?

Or is it just that I don't remember
those things
and no one ever told me again
Until they're telling someone else
I need****** this I just use******* not too. —

---

*   Like,
**   do
***   what they told me
**** overlook
***** why did
******to do
*******choose

14   It makes no sense
2/20/19

It's a little water
Put a little shampoo in the hair
Washing around a little bit
Put a little more water in
And let it be clean

It's a little water
Put a little Body soap on the body
Wash yourself till you're clean
You empty out the water
And your whole body is clean

Then why is it so hard
I don't want to touch the body with
the water
'Want to wash the hair it's scary
Feel like I can't breathe
Don't know what happened to make it
change that way —

15   Frustrating
2/27/19

I am happy most of the times
*Feel good most of the time
**Can laugh sometimes when it's funny
***Do something silly and giggle about it

But sometimes I get tired of being
repetitive
I get tired of not understanding and trying
to figure it out
I get frustrated because I don't understand
And sometimes I want to cry but I can't
even do that

And what's even more sad
Is I can't even explain it to anyone
What's going on or how to fix it or to
even understand
You just keep going and going. —

---

*   I
**   I
***   I

16   Please slow down!
4/17/19

My words are different
And I'm* very hard
To figure out what to say
Or how to answer a question

I can't do all my chores
In just a day a week or a month
I can't understand books
But I can read the words

It** sad that I can still get lost
But I'm trying to get better
I mostly stay at home all the time
Because it's hard for other*** to understand

I try to share aphasia with other people
The church and my friends are great
at understanding
But I have had many professional people
That don't seem to understand
and that**** sad

Please take care of people with aphasia
Please just slow down
Give us a chance
We are smart people! —

---

*   it's
**   in the brain
***   people
****   it is

17 Repetitively
6/7/19

Repetition
Random routines
Redundant
Habitual
Learn
Relearn
Persistent
Learn and Relearn

As a little child
Going to school every day
ABC's
123
I pledge allegiance
We learn and relearn every day
Until we get them right

With Aphasia and a stroke
With therapy and life
Learning ABC's again
Learning 123's again
Learning words again
And we learn and relearn again
And now we try not to lose it —

18   Aphasia Music
6/14/2019

"S" can read one or two words at a time.
"D" can show us but we can't hardly read what he says.

We have a lot of time learning new words and letters.
And we have different ways we need to learn.

It's hard and will take a long time to do it.
But music really does help!

Because music is on the other side of the brain
We can read with music!

"S", "D", me and so many others
Can read the music all the time!!

It is just a wonderful thing
To be able to keep the music going!!! —

19 Am I being whiny?
7/15/19

I want to do what God asks me to
And I try to understand how to with Aphasia

So why is it I don't understand how to do things?
Or many things I just don't remember anymore.

And if I happen to learn something new
It's like something else goes away!

My Aphasia and my diabetes Are important
I am trying very hard to learn to take care of them

Then I have husband animals house food laundry...*
Then somewhere in there my shower nails done hair and cloth

Then somewhere there are the many doctors appointments
I don't even want to get started on that

I just don't know how to do it all and I pray every day
God please just get me through this one day at a time —

---

*   chores

20   Friend-less
8/8/19

I have asked God so many times
For the people that I love are hurting
Or need help I think they can't do alone
And I think I do a lot to try to help other people

But I have recently* some of my help
People don't want to do what you supposed do
And now they are walking away from me
What do I do with that God? How do I pray? —

---

*   got

21 It changes you
11/7/19

Sometimes I don't want to learn anymore
You get tired
and you worry
And you get sad

When I first had my stroke
I laughed a lot
And everything was funny
And I was never sad

I didn't worry about anything
And wrong words didn't make me mad
Learning how to do things
I just didn't know

Now I worry about my kids
I worry about my dad
I worry about my husband
I worry about everybody

I used to want to be able to do everything
But all that does is make me worry
Makes me feel like I can't do it anything right
Makes me wish I was back at the beginning —

22   My Dad's Life after a Stroke
11/26/19

My dad had many friends
They used to go to the "V"*
Talking and laughing and have a few beers
Come visit the house once in a while

One day he went to the "V"
And he told his friend Steve:
"I'm not feeling too good"
And Steve said "I'm not understanding things to"**

So Steve took him to the hospital
They said he had a stroke
They moved him to Nashville
And The next day he went home

Steve checked on him every day
He has some therapy
And some PT
And usually doing much better

He used to go to the "V"
Even when Steve had to move
But no one else from the "V"
Never came to his house

---

*   VFW
** with Dad

Now He seems so lonely
He just has his routine
His sister-in-law visits
Maybe every two weeks

He goes to Walmart
And to La Cazona
To the doctors appointments
Calls family

But it's so lonely
All day long
Just the TV
And him..... —

23   Sometimes Adult, sometimes a Child
12/14/19

I have things I'm supposed to do as an adult
And I try to do them good* most the time
But there's so much I would much like to be a child
Enjoy your things at all would have

I know I'm supposed to clean and cook
And make everything look nice
But I rather play with babies
And toys and have a good time

So many other things I don't remember anymore
But so much new things I would like to do
But as you're supposed to be an adult every day
How can you play with others as a child

My life is different now with the changes
And I know many think they don't treat you differently
But it happens every day
Not much fun but I played by myself —

---

   *   well

24   thought it was better but not
12/31/19

I was talking to a cousin
About Christmas and kids
And sharing a picture
From a few years ago

When she said she missed her dad
This was her first year he was done
And I thought to myself has he
passed away
Or was he in healthcare* now?

So why couldn't I remember
the answer?
It's so important why can't I
remember?
I tried to ask my husband and
he said he thought he passed
But I had to look it up in my
own information** to look it up!

I was sad and upset because I
couldn't remember and had to
look it up
Although I understand why it
happens
I sometimes think it's better
and it's not
I'll always have this problem
and I just need to learn. —

---

*   home health
**   computer

25   Sad and frustrated
1/23/2020

       I think this is one of the worst things
       That really frustrates me
       My pictures are so important to me
       And now they're hard for me to find them all

       I thought I had kept them altogether for years
       Because they're everybody I've ever cared about and loved
       But now I can't even find them all
       And it makes me sad to* share them all

       So I get sorry that I have** a stroke
       And things I can't find anymore
       And I'm frustrated and I'm sad
       To Not be able share it with you who is so important —

---

*   not be able to
** had

26   What are your feelings/opinions about COVID-19?
4/3/2020

Well my feelings or opinions may be different than most people.
I see so many people worried about money
Or worried that other people are saying 6 feet away
Or other people not doing what people are worried about doing
And that is sad that they spend their time worrying about other people

Then there's many people that have been very helpful
Providing food and toilet paper and Medicine
Saying hello to them at a safe distance
Just to say hi and say we are still here

Yes people have been sick
And some people have died
But many have recovered
And many more will in the future

But what I saw was a chance for agape love
To care about other people and what they need
To understand those of us that live this day every day
And how we learn to take care of each other

Yes it's hard but we take care of each other
And God takes care of us
And in the end
This too shall pass —

27   Memory has been gone forever
6/5/2020

I have loved my kids all my life
I* really meant everything to me
I thought I was really good at it
But I wasn't as good as it seemed

My husband and I have been friends forever
We've known each other since high school
I thought I was really good at taking care of you** every day
But I wasn't as good as it seemed

I love my mom and dad beyond measure every day
They did everything to take care of me till I grew up
I thought I took good care of them later
But I wasn't as good as it seemed

I don't remember the many things my kids tell me about
I don't remember the many things my husband tells me about
I don't remember taking care of my mom as best as I could
Because I've lost many things that I have remembered

And now I have*** a stroke when I was 58
I still love my kids with all my heart
I still love my husband with all my heart
My mom passed away but my dad is still living and I love him
But there are still only certain things I can't**** remember the rest goes away. —

---

*   It
**   him
***   had
****   can

28   Empty stroke
06/23/2020

When I had my stroke the left part of my brain became empty
I really didn't know the people that were around me but somehow I knew I loved them
I was very happy to just be able to spend time with each other
I didn't have anything at that time that I had to do

As time moved on and I got some speech therapy and some walking therapy
I tried to learn more about who I was and the things I used to like to do
I remembered my job and I missed it a lot and house and grandkids
But those really weren't things I could do anything with anymore

But I really tried to work on cleaning the house and cooking for the family
I tried keeping in touch with people I'm trying to [hear from]* them and call them
I really tried doing all the things that I used to do to take care of other people
But I'm really not good at it anymore and my body just gets too tired

---

*   write

I really enjoy my therapy and my learning to read books and the Bible
I really enjoy my music and how it makes me feel to sing
I really enjoy the people when we are able to talk about strokes with each other
But it's not made to have it every single day to enjoy

I don't know how to not be the person to clean and cook on* the house
And keeping up with people and calling
And I would like to just do therapy and get better every day
But it just doesn't seem what other's want every day

So I try a little bit of cleaning and a little bit of therapy
A little bit of cooking and a little bit of grandkids
Add a little bit more of therapy with music in** the Bible
But I get so tired every day I can't get it all done.

And then I get frustrated because I just want to work on myself
I just want my therapy to try to get better every day
I know that I am not the same person I used to be
And I just wish everyone else would understand that and let me be me. —

---

*   at
**   and

29 Dab nab it I did it again!
7/17/2020

This is really something
That aggravate the death out of me

Since I've had my stroke
I don't drive

So most of my wishes
Are done online

I like curtains and Books
(even though I'm just learning again to read)

I'd like nice things in the kitchen
And extras in the bed and bathroom

But I ordered a doll
And it came to be 3 inches

I ordered pots and pans
And they came in as fingernail clippers

I ordered three pushrods
To go with some wonderful curtains

The pushrods are shower curtains
And of course they're way too long

I still have other things that are coming
I don't know what they'll look like then

But it seems I work so hard for it
And it's still not the right things

And I just can't understand it
How to make it better —

30   Life after a stroke
7/27/2020

What does a person do with their life after a stroke?
Many times you can't drive, your speech is a different life.
You don't really see a lot of people or friends that you used to.
You are called retired now but that just means you can't work.

We used to go out with our friends to movies or restaurants.
We used to go out and play with our kids and our grandkids and enjoy.
We used to go out and see different and amazing things we haven't* seen before.
Our spouses used to hold our hands and go out to spend time with each other.

Now sometimes we have a caregiver that takes care of us.
Sometimes our spouse goes to work all day and we are home.
Maybe someone comes and cleans the house maybe not.
A friend may call on the phone but then again maybe not.

So then what is there to do every day that keeps you going?
Do you sometimes just talk to yourself how do you say nothing at all?
And when you have somebody to talk to you do you talk too much?
Then sometimes they may get angry or upset!

---

*   hadn't

I know that God says there is a place for me.
I just haven't found that place yet and I don't just want to be a blip on the wall.
I don't want to be here just because somebody doesn't want to say goodbye.
I just want to know where is my place now after my life with a stroke? —

31   Changing the bed after a stroke

I have to take the dirty bedsheets out
And then the other ones I want to put on the bed
Also have to be washed because they've been there for a while.
So while they're washing I try to turn the mattress.
Well I could almost do it but I needed one more person
Because I have a California king mattress.
So it didn't happen I just turn the mattress around.

After the sheets have done drying
I take all the pillows and put them in the dryer with a bounce
Trying to make them smell nice and pretty.
But we have lots of pillows so I have to do it twice.
Then I put some Fabreeze all over them
To make sure they smelled good!

Then I go and put the new sheets on the mattress
And make sure they are all tucked in nice and tight.
Then I go put in all the pillows and where they go
and make sure I put Azhra in his spot!
Then I put our blankets where each one goes
And it makes it look so much nice and pretty.

Then I put in my stuffed animals
That belong right with my pillows
As they're important to me and sometimes at
night they keep me company.
And after I have finished that is* naptime!

I started this today at 7:30 AM.
I spent 30 minutes with my husband for lunch
I have been working at this The rest of that time.
And I finished it at 2:00 PM.
After a nap we have to clean our self up first!! —

---

*   it's

32   I am different now
       than four years ago today
       8/20/2020

I have worked for 20 years, been pretty busy taking care of things, my husband and I have four kids along with many other kids that we have help taking care of over the years, grandkids who I love just beyond measure. We've had our ups and downs but most the time we were happy every day.

Are used to love to write and journal a lot. And I was pretty good at numbers to I could take care of my own taxes along with all the good stuff I did with work that required a lot of writing and numbers. I was really helpful with taking care of other people through my work and it was great.

Oh and I used to love to read books a lot! I loved a lot of them but my favorite that I used to read was Stephen king! Long time ago it was something me and my mom could read together and I used to get tickled at her reading in the evening and hollering to her " mom mom mom" and she was engrossed in her book she couldn't even hear me!

Many people might say my life was nothing great but you know it was to me! I have a husband who I love beyond measure and my kids are all grown up I'm doing great to take care of the room and my grandkids call me Nana which makes me very happy. I could go places and I worked and I had great friends and had given my life to God and it was great!!

And then, on August 20 2016, Life changed and my husband found me that morning after I had a stroke.

I don't drive now I can't even ride a bicycle so I can't go anywhere without help for other people. I can't write and turn on like I used to, writing a couple sentences at a time is all I can get. I wasn't able to read books for the longest time but I'm really getting better it's just very very slow and they're very very short. They tell me I will never work

again and I really miss the people. My numbers I am not good at at all I can't even figure them out half the time. And sometimes understanding what people say I can't figure it out either it's better if you write it down for me. I use a recording for most of my writing and it helps me with numbers as well.

Yes, I can stay home by myself now most of the time. And my husband has helped me figure out how to make some foods for us that I can do OK with but figuring it out on my own as hard. And I take care of my animals most of the time by myself. And I try to take care of the house as best I can but not like I used to because I get tired easily. And being alone all the time it's sad.

So yes I know my life has changed a lot and I know but the only reason I'm here is God has a plan I just don't know where it is yet. But I really would like people around me to know that my life is changed and please don't treat me like I used to be because I'm not. I am a different person now and I'm more like a child learning life all over again and it can be fun when I'm not trying to fight trying to make myself be something I'm not anymore. I just keep trying to work on it good or bad it's just me.

33   Untitled
9/12/2020

Many years ago I had left eye dominant eyes.
I was really good with a gun with a bow and arrow.
In my left eye was my good eye.
My right eye had issues And had to have glasses.

Then, in about 1990 Or so, I had retinal occlusion.
So I lost my left Good Eye.
Been an interesting time [morning have]* to move around with it.
But my life was really hard then and we didn't play guns and stuff.
And then I went to work my time for 20 years doing that.

August 20, 2016 I had a major stroke and I have Aphasia.
Sometimes things are hard to not understand now.
We went to go do some shooting today.
And I cannot blink eye, I had to use my right hand now.

---

*   learning how

It was so hard to figure out how to do that.
Need to keep doing it the way it* supposed to be done.
My body kept trying to do the left.
Do** use right eye to work*** was really hard to figure out now.

But I will have to keep working to have to learn more.
As I want to get better like I used to be.
My spouse says I did a really good job.
It was just really hard to learn it new.

I don't know if there are ways to learn things in a better way.
Today sometimes I could feel my brain having a hard time learning.
I don't know if others could understand that or not.
But I will keep working at it because I really want to be better.
—

---

*   it's
**   To
***   shoot

34   This is what sad in Life now.

"There is really something that
used to be up here before you clean
this room, where might it be?"

"I don't remember being anything up there before,
I am very sorry"

"Well it wasn't that long ago that you cleaned it up!"

"It seems like forever ago!" Looking!!

I still don't know where it is.

Are things my brain loses, in my memory goes away. —

35   What Jesus teaches us and then what we do
10/12/2020

I see people stealing other peoples children.
It's so sad and angry and hurtful
I don't understand how people can do those things.
It's not what Jesus teaches us.

I see the news of other people killing other people.
And I don't understand it killing other families.
To be hurtful and selfish, it makes no sense to me.
And that's not what Jesus teaches us.

I see children fighting children with each other.
Just because this is what they want to have.
I don't understand who teaches them this things.
Because that's not what Jesus teaches us.

I see spouses being ugly to each other constantly.
How can you expect someone to love you being ugly all the time?
If that's how you talk to each other how do you love each other!
That's not what Jesus teaches us

And then when you go to worship and you see someone hurting someone.
I don't understand at all how anyone could do that!
We are supposed to love like Jesus loves!
That's what Jesus teaches us!—

36   Lost forever
12/24/2020

My important ornaments
My stocking* on the tree
My Christmas Eve pajamas
My extras left for my little kids
They are gone
For the four years
Each Christmas one disappears
I can't figure out where they might go
I have cleaned every closet
And cleaned every bed
There** like your brain after a stroke
It*** puts it**** in a hidden box
And it***** may never ever come out —

---

*   mini-stockings
**   They are
***   My brain
**** the lost items
***** the lost items

37   I don't like being "me" anymore
3/12/2021

I used to have my own thoughts
In my own feelings
And I could spend time taking care
Of what needed each day
And no one really said much to me

But now I've had a stroke
And I have to get help
With like medicine and doctors appointments
And my words and my language is different
And so it requires a lot of help from other people

But what I don't understand now
Is when does that help
Decide to change who you are?
To just stop doing something
Because someone says don't do it anymore?

I'm a very caring person I think
I love people and I want to see them and talk to them
I love birds and sugar gliders
And I love cats and I love dogs both very much
So when do you decide to just walk away from them?

When does somebody else decide
They are causing a problem for you
And you just need to stop doing it
And walk away from it like you don't care?
Sure makes me not want to be here anymore! —

38   Every day always
4/18/21

You have two people together
A working man
His legs always hurting
But he works every day
A used to work wife
She has a stroke
And other issues in the body

Who cleans your house?
Who picks up the trash?
Who does the dishes?
Who does the laundry?
Who takes care of the animals?
Who does any of it?

We are just different people
And we care about different things
some rest a lot
And watch TV
And others clean for everyone
And care about what they need
Then life goes on... —

39   How do you decide?
4/21/21

The spouse-
Oh my God my loved one had a stroke!
They're asleep I pray they wake up!
I need you to live because I love you!!
I need to take care of you and provide for you!
Then as you get better there is just so much more!
Like Chores dishes laundry taking care of my things!
It's all because I love you!

The stroke-
I never knew I was asleep. Waking up was nice.
Don't remember anything but many people care about me.
I knew everyone was important I just didn't know why.
I did everything they asked me to do actually got a little bit better.
Then it became do I do therapy or do I do other chores?
Which one is more important?
I can't do both? which one? which one?
Well I try to work on both because
I really love you and I have to take care of me! —

40   Hurting heart
5/6/21

How do you take care of your heart
When your kids hearts are hurting?
When your grandkids have been hurt
And your help was just not enough?
When they hurt so bad it makes Them angry?
And even the words make you hurt?
Seems like there's nothing you can do
To teach them ways to get through it.
Many people just say walk away.
But you know it can't be fixed
But maybe we can look at it a different way
And take it to a healing place. —

41   When your heart is hurting
5/21/21

My heart is hurting
And I just want it to stop

Upsetting people
And I don't always understand why

People are different
Many can just be mean

I used to be a fighter
But they fought so hard now

Anything to try to make you
Be what they want you to be

They fight you to give up everything
That are important to me

Sometimes I just want to give up
And I just don't wanna fight any more

I just want my heart hurting
And the only way to do that is to go home —

5/18/21
Bye miss blest and ROFLS —

42   Hurt Someone
5/21/21

I really hurt my husband
I didn't mean to
I was worried about my own self
I didn't think about what would hurt him

Now his heart is hurting
And he doesn't want to talk to me now
And I can't even tell him
But it wasn't about him

It's about me and my life
And how I feel these days
My brain just doesn't work like it used to
And sometimes it's very sad

But it doesn't matter now
Because his heart is hurting
And it's because I caused it
And I can't make it better —

43 People
5/27/21

I watch people since my stroke
I watch them at therapy and star
I watch him on Facebook and on the Internet
Watching what people are like with other people

I have watched people during their strokes and other injuries
And the couples are together
and they love each other very much
And the one with the stroke/injury is taking such good care of the other person
And it's a wonderful thing to see together

I have watched people during their strokes and other injuries
And the couples how together and they love each other very much
And one with the stroke/injury has lots of problems
And the other person is very angry and very hurtful towards them

I have watched other people during the stroke and other injuries
And I have seen couples that don't love each other anymore
A person with the stroke/injury is left alone by the other person who leaves
And they are both left alone hurting and sad

I have watched people bring their strokes and other injuries
And I don't understand the difference people are
Some are wonderful some are happy and some are very sad
I don't understand how people can be different people that love —

44 Aphasia and the Bible
6/29/21

I love to listen to the Bible
The problem is that if it's not written down
Many of it I can't understand any more
I can't read from someone else
Deuteronomy or a Genesis or Titus
And then I can't read numbers like
Like 25 or 40 or even 15
So many times if someone can help
I can find my way in the Bible
But if I'm by myself I get lost
And I get sad and really depressed
Many times I pray
Dear heavenly father please
Help me learn to find a way to
Do this with you
Because this is my life now and it's very hard
And I just want other people to know.

45   Untitled
7/12/21

I took my little brain out today
And I put it in a basket
It went to see other people
And get to know their life

So I went to the doctor's office
And he said I've told you this before
My brain looked at him and said
She told you I am broken.

So I went to see my kids today
And they told me they weren't gonna be here
My brain looked at them and said
She told you I am broken.

So I went to be helpful today
And they told me they don't want my help
My brain looked at them and said
She told you I am broken.

I picked up my little brain
And I padded little head
And I told my little brain
We'll be broken together. —

46 Clouds
7/21/21

I love to look up in the sky
And see what's up there to see
Sometimes I can see an airplane flying
Sometimes I see the birds beautiful
I often see the sunshine and it's warm
But the beautiful clouds
They seem fluffy and soft
And they have shapes and colors
And some are gray and some are blue
And sometimes I get dark and scary
But laying in the grass and
Looking up into the sky
It is so peaceful and so quiet
I just feel so good. —

47   Routine – Change
7/26/21

I get up in the morning
Help my husband get ready for work
I take my medicine with my boost
I read my Bible and my study

Then I make up what I'm gonna do
To do for the rest of the day
Taking care of my Ashra
I'm taking care of the house

Then I have 10 birds to take care of
Sometimes they're hard to take care of
Get them food and water
And clean up their cages

I also have 17 sugar gliders to take care of
And they are interesting to do
They get special food and get them plenty of water
I clean their cages but it's hard
It takes me all day to do what I'm gonna do

So then when I get another thing to add
Turn my routine upside down
And I had to figure out how to fit it in

I have my routine and it was all right
So how do I fit this more than one in
Three days it has been all out of whack
And I have to get it back together again. —

48   STINKS!
8/16/21

I had surgery on my arm
And now it has a cast
Then I haven't been feeling good
And I can't clean The house
And it STINKS!!

I can't wash the dishes
I can't vacuum the floors
I can't mop the kitchen
Can't hardly even take a bath!

I have a new doggy
It's a little name is Lucas
He has not learned to go outside
And he really doesn't like to listen
And he loves the hallway!

The smell is really bothering me
It really makes me want to cry
And I want to try to fix it
But I broke my other elbow trying
So right now I just be whining! —

49   Remember the great things
8/24/21

Been thinking a lot lately
And my mind just goes and goes
There are many things that I am proud I have done
And then there are many things
I feel I have lost

I had my first living baby
When I was 16.
I'm thankful for my parents
And all their love for me.

I graduated high school
And I am very proud of that!
And I graduated early
And that is just a wonderful thing

I married my high school sweetheart
And he is a wonderful man
He works very hard to take care of me
And he just works the best he can

We had four living kids together
And we did the best we could
Yes we had our problems
But my love would never change

I went to College later
And I enjoyed it so much
I learned great things
I was thankful when I graduated!

And then I found this wonderful job
And I stayed with it forever
And I thought I would be able to stay until I would retire
But unfortunately it was not to be but I still love it

Oh those are many of the wonderful things I love
They're all the things that I will never forget
But it's sad that the brain remembers
All the things that are sad, angry or hurt

There are things in my life I have hurt my husband
And I think about them often and wish I could take them away
I can't believe I can do those things
But it stays here every day

There are things in my life that my husband has hurt me
And I try not to bring about him very often
But sometimes they stay in my brain
And I don't know how to make it stop

I have a daughter whose heart is hurting
Something someone else said
It was supposed to be helping me
But hurt her and it stays

I have a son we don't see anymore
Many things have happened
But I pray all things are good
But he is hurt as well

I have two tiny babies
That we will never see
It's sad that I did that
I wish I had known Jesus then

Our other daughter and son
With all that they have
They still stay with us
And love us through everything

I have many grandkids
And a few great grandkids
I don't see them very often
But I'm thankful to have them

It seems so much has gone away
And I know all the things I have done
Mostly made me who I am today
But I want to remember the great things the most. —

50   Words or lack there of
9/20/21

Words are hard
Many I can't understand
It makes a conversation uneasy
It makes learning hard
Makes reading difficult
And so I just try to stay away from it —

51 I learned something new
9/27/21

I went to a restaurant
With some wonderful people
They've been helping me
Since I first had my stroke
A little over five years ago.

I was trying to decide
What I was going to get to drink
And it often takes me a while
To put my words together
Tell the waitress what to drink.

I told the waitress
I have a stroke
Please give me a minute
And I will get it together
And tell you what it will be.

Then I heard one of my family
Say directly to me
"it's been too long since the stroke,
You can't use that anymore."
I was devastated!

I never thought I'd hear that
Come from the people
That I love
I thought we had learned so much
About stroke and Aphasia

I have learned to hear that
Some people I don't know
Say things like that
But I never thought
It would come from them. —

52 Quiet
10/11/21

Sometimes Things I don't understand.
Sometimes I ask a question
And sometimes I don't understand their answer.
And sometimes they're saying
"Well you're telling me I'm supposed to".
When I just wanted to know are you going?
I don't know what's wrong with me
That makes it be that way.
It makes me where I don't want to
Talk, ask questions, answers or stories.
I would just rather be quiet
And look at Facebook.
And it's always quiet. T.V or radio.
When they never have nothing to say.
I always wonder why am I here?
Everybody wanted me to always be here.
But why? They really don't talk to me or ask me what am I thinking.
Or what am I doing or learning.
Just get medicine or go to the doctor, don't get lost, don't go anywhere.
I know my friend is Jesus, and I sure wish He would tell me why I'm still here. I'm sure I could do a good job. —

53 Future
10/14/21

I don't drive
I don't go to the grocery store
I don't pay the electricity or the gas
I don't pay house taxes
I don't pay car insurance

I do take care of my animals
I try to make lunch and dinner,
most of the time
I try to clean the house,
I'm very slow at it
I do the dishes,
Keep them clean
The toilets are nice,
and usable
I do all the laundry,
Sometimes one day sometimes two
I do vacuuming,
All through the house.
I do mopping in the kitchen,
And laundry room
And I work outside,
Clean up and garden
I do to STAR,
Once a week
I go to therapy
Once a week
Sometimes doctors appointments,
It just takes a while

I pay my own bills,
Once a month
I pay my medical insurance,
Once a month
I am learning to read
My writing is hard
My brain doesn't catch up on a lot of things
Am I walking is just different sometimes
And life has been very different
But I am still here
I have a hard time understanding
And sometimes I'm happy
Sometimes I'm very sad
But every day I am thankful
That I am still here
And I look forward to
who I will be in the future —

54. Are you trusting and who do you trust?
10/25/21

Are you a trusting person?
Do you think your parents would trust you?
Do you think your spouse would trust you?
Do you think your kids would trust you?

And then do you you trust your parents?
How do you trust your spouse?
Do you get disabled I still trust?
And do you trust your kids?

Do you have a best friend and trust them?
Do you have someone walking down the street do you trust them?
Do you have someone running do your backyard do you trust them?

How do we learn to trust other people?
Or do we only trust certain people?
How do we learn to be trusted?
How do we learn to be trusted to get better?

Have you ever thought you'd learn to trust
Only to find you're really not trusted
As much as you thought?
Think about it quite often now, did we ever have it or not? —

55   Small Stuff
12/16/2021

Things are lost
Memories are gone
Some of the words are coming back
Writing them down with words,
It's like a child and being slow.
It's five years since I had a stroke
And living with Aphasia
And if it's not sitting in front of me
Then I don't remember it
And memories go away
I needed my cover ID card
I knew I had it
my husband said it was important
I looked and looked all over
just don't remember where it was at
It's one of many things
That I can't seem to find these days
But today I prayed to God
Please Lord if it is your will
There's many things that I can't find
I know you know where they are
My husband says I need it
So please can you help me find it
And Jesus name I pray amen
And then I sat down for a little bit
And something came and told me
"come look on your desk"
And that paper was in those!!
God will provide even the small stuff —

56 Thank you for the joy
1/24/2022

Today we day goodbye
To my sweetest sugar gliders.
They mean the world
And they're so kind
And really silly
And boy they could bite too!
We made mamas and daddies
And sweet little babies.
I enjoyed feeding you
I'm giving you treats
Like chicken and Cheerios.
And now it's time to say goodbye
And you're gonna go live with Mr. Ryan
And he and his friends.
They'll take care of you
And you continue with a wonderful life.

57 Aphasia and life
1/25/2022

Is your life different with a Aphasia?

Do you have a spouse you also like to acre for since you have a Aphasia?

Maybe with Aphasia do you have children or pets that you care for or try to?

Since you have a Aphasia do you have someone who helps you with the chores or do you do it?

Since you have a Aphasia do you have a job, do you have a spouse that also has a job?

Do you do the chores outside or do you have someone else do those since you have a Aphasia?

Since you have a Aphasia are you able to drive or do you need help to get around?

Do you have a caregiver since you have aphasia that goes with you through speech therapy? Or does a spouse go or do you do it alone?

With having Aphasia, is there at any time of anything you have needed or would you like to do, have you chose not to do it because you didn't want to ask the other person or you're trying to care for them more, is there just too much to do and it's only you to do it and so you can't take care of the Aphasia too?

Just trying to figure out do some of us stop doing our aphasia to do life things instead...

Just something to think about

58   A valentine for my husband
2/11/2022

To my husband, Kevin, Who I love more than life itself

We have been friends for 48 years. And we have been married for
45 years, in two months.

We have four living children, 13 grandchildren and three great grandchildren.

And there are many more adopted grandchildren that we love beyond measure.

We haven't been perfect. Many times we have both been mean to each other. And right now I can't even tell you why we would even do that.

But right now it seems to me, my sweet husband, that you are not happy, you seem very sad.

Even before your body hurt, it seems you've had stopped wanting to do anything. It's like nothing makes you feel better.

It's been this way for several years and I don't know how to fix it. I just wanted you to know about it and that I pray our heavenly father will take care of it with you.

Yes I know I am a different person now, and I'm sorry about that. But that has not changed how much I love you, spending my life with you and hoping that you will be happy.

I pray every day that whatever it is you need that will make you feel better that God will provide! And I do mean whatever God thinks you need!

I love you Kevin, and I wish you a happy Valentine's Day. —

59   Overdrive on the brain
3/9/2022

Do you find a word,
Or a picture maybe,
Or maybe even a thought
Or a cause even
And it just continues to stay

And stay and stay and stay.

You need to move on.
To do your next chore
Or study or thought
Let it just stays and stays

And I keep working on it and
Thinking on it and looking at it
And studying it.
Trying to figure it out.

While it stays and stays and stays. —

60   The Letter L
4/4/2022

LaDonna
LaDonna loves Jesus
LaDonna gives her life to her husband
LaDonna worries about all her children
LaDonna lavishes over her grandchildren
LaDonna is so blessed by great grandchildren
LaDonna is so thankful that her dad is still living
LaDonna is thankful her mother gave her this name. —

61 Not Matching-Matching Aphasia
4/19/2022

806-522-9656
806-491-5691
Nope not matching
Just keep trying

Romans 8:29? Nope
Romans 8:18? Nope
Romans 8:28? Yay!
Just trying to figure out what I asked for I'm trying to make it match!

Aphasia is hard sometimes to figure out what someone is asking me or what I'm trying to find.
It's hard to find what's matching and what is not on numbers and letters.
I'm thankful for my speech therapy friends that help me try to learn! —

62 Life is different now.
4/27/22

I am disabled.
I had a stroke,
And I have aphasia.
"Aphasia, loss of language NOT intellect".
I'm married and raised four kids.
I went to college later in life, then had a job for almost 20 years.
But now I'm not good with numbers, nor with words.
Driving by myself is not an option, I use a bus to get around.
So a job is out of the question.
I love going to church to spend time with my church family!
I have caregivers that help me often times.
But I really enjoy helping other people.
Getting things done that are very helpful.
And they remind me how GOOD Jesus is.
But I'm not able to help other people much, I guess it's because of my disability.
I can't help them with money because mine pays all my bills.
So it's hard to figure out where you are in life, just living day by day.
When wondering where to be in five years, it will still all be the same.
"Aphasia, loss of language not intellect"; but wondering for me WHAT will make a difference? —

63   Different
6/23/2022

Just because you can't see it.
My body is not paralyzed.
My legs work enough.
My arms can move around.
I am able to make some dinner.
And tell people I love them.
Smile at them every day.
And try to help them out.

I cannot drive a car.
I cannot go for a walk,
Unless I have a friend.
I cannot go grocery shopping alone.
The TV is too noisy, hard to understand.
Reading is hard and takes much time.
Talking on the phone is hard.
And too many people talking make brain hurt.

Yes, life is getting better.
But it's very tiring!
Just to get up every day,
Takes so much work just to keep going.
To think keeps the brain going,
A bazillion miles a minute!
And it goes constantly day and night.
When does it ever stop?

See, my brain is broken.
A piece of it is missing.
I had a stroke that gave me aphasia:
It's a loss of language not intelligence.
Which means every minute of every day it's Life is hard!
I will never be the person that used to be.
I am different. Still loving and caring, just changing to be different. —

64 Trial: Poems on Speech — Inner Speech/Aphasia Conflict
6/27/22

Talking to oneself internally,
A little verbal conversation.
Few words or full sentences,
Just to ask or answer questions.
May make sense, it may not.
Sometimes they're just "there".
But you know that's hard to do
When you have aphasia.
Most of the time it needs to be quiet.
Noises, sounds, animals, people
make things hard to understand.
Radio, Music, TV and YouTube,
Fills that brain up fuller and Fuller.
So how do you work on your inner speech?
How do we talk to our inner self?
It's not like it used to be before Aphasia,
When we used to do it all the time without even thinking.
So now we have to remember
To make a quiet time.
To walk away from the noise that fills our brain.
So that we can listen to what it says;
    I need to remember to take my medicine.
    Oh I made a mess today.
    Oh fluffy fluffy.
    Oh things I don't understand.
    And so many more our brain talks to us for. —

65   Aphasia hamburger helper
7/13/22

Apparently I was having a brain problem yesterday.
I was making hamburger helper X two.
Hamburger was already ready from the day before, so that was great!
I put in the noodles
And I put in the sauce. Good job!
Then I looked up how much water and I got 5 cups.
What!! How did you figure out why cups? And you've already put them all in there!!
Well then I needed to have some milk. It said 4 cups. But I had already put way too much water in there...
So, I only needed 2 1/2 cups of water, But there was two more, so that's about five, so I only put 2 cups of milk.
I think the liquid was about the same I just really prayed that would taste good for my husband.
I have really seem to enjoy it and I didn't tell him about the mess I made.
I am just going to call my Aphasia moment. —

66   Lucas and Bailey
9/8/2022

A little boy named Lucas,
Moved into this house.
He was so happy
I need loved to play!

Playing out back,
Lucas met a little boy
In the left neighborhood
I will two of them play all the time!!

Then on another day,
Lucas met another boy
In the right neighborhood,
His name was Buck.

Buck needed food and water
And someone to care for him.
But Lucas played Play with him

While we tried to find him a home.

Buck had another friend
In the right neighborhood .
It was a little girl
And she was stuck in a crate.

Their family were not very nice
And they treat people pretty Mean.
But we did the best we could provide food and water.
And lots of love!

One day Lucas came out to play
And Buck was gone!!
We couldn't find him anywhere!
We saw he was picked up by the Animal Shelter.

But the little girl was out of the crate.
She was so pretty and sweet.
We put her food in her yard.
And Lucas talk to her every day.

She learned to get out of the fence
and get in Lucas' yard
And boy howdy!!
Lucas had a great day!!
She would come to see him every day.
And she would have plenty of food and water.
And lots and lots of love!
We gave her the name Bailey.

She came every day
Several times a day

Lucas and Bailey played and played
And then they continued played more!

Lucas would run out the door
He would call Bailey Bailey!
And she would come running!
They did this for months!!

And they had so much fun!!
And I got to where they would just sit together
looking around
Just being the best friends!!

Then one day last week
Bailey came for breakfast
They came to play
Then that afternoon she didn't come back.

Lucas cried and cried!
He says Bailey Bailey!!
Where are you??
He has looking everywhere!

I don't know how to tell him
They probably took her somewhere else.
That she was took away.
He will probably see her again.

But his little heart is hurting
And he cries every day.
Still looking to see
This is coming around around the corner.

We pray every day
Wherever Bailey may be,
She will be in a good home
Where someone will love her unconditionally!! —

67 Black Hole
10/10/22

When you fell asleep
Your words and numbers
Went away
They were lost
In space and time
And distance far away
When you woke up
You looked around
What's your name?
Who are you?
I need something
But how do I say it?
They have turned into
The big black hole
I need a Star Trek captain
To dig them out
to find them words
And put them back again
Away from the black hole. —

68   Ending 2019
12/31/19

This is been a wonderful year
God has blessed me with so much
He has blessed me with family
That I love infinity and beyond
He has blessed me with the time to get to visit people
To meet my first great grandson's
To spend time with my dad still
Which I am so blessed
And God is changing me
 I think it's such a good way
I'm just really thankful for everything he does
Continue prayers for all of you every day
And I look forward to 2020
And all the things God blessed us with! —

69   Sometimes Adult, sometimes a Child
12/14/19

I have things I'm supposed to do as an adult
And I try to do them good most the time
But there's so much I would much like to be a child
Enjoy your things at all would have

I know I'm supposed to clean and cook
And make everything look nice
But I rather play with babies
And toys and have a good time

So many other things I don't remember anymore
But so much new things I would like to do
But as you're supposed to be an adult every day
How can you play with others as a child

My life is different now with the changes
And I know many think they don't treat you differently
But it happens every day
Not much fun but I played by myself —

70   It changes you
11/7/19

Sometimes I don't want to learn anymore
You get tired
and you worry
And you get sad

When I first had my stroke
I laughed a lot
And everything was funny
And I was never sad

I didn't worry about anything
And wrong words didn't make me mad
Learning how to do things
I just didn't know

Now I worry about my kids
I worry about my dad
I worry about my husband
I worry about everybody

I used to want to be able to do everything
But all that does is make me worry
Makes me feel like I can't do it anything right
Makes me wish I was back at the beginning —

71 Short Story-essay

I lived in Virginia near Hampton
I was about in the fifth grade it was during the summer
I thought my parents were mean to my Brother very much so
I decided I was going to run away and had a friend that would go with me
We had on shorts and T-shirts and no shoes
I thought that if I was gone my parents would be nicer to my brother
Well the two of us walked in the woods for hours and hours
At one time we found a little school place to get something to drink
Then we walked farther and the policeman came and picked us up
It's the first time I've ever walked in a police man car
They took us home to our parents
And I got the weapon of my life —

72   Dream
1/26/2020

2 more strokes-
Asking what to do
No more medicine
Try to make it move faster
Trying to help Kevin

Then woke up —

73 Lost forever
12/24/2020

My important ornaments
My stocking on the tree
My Christmas Eve pajamas
My extras left for my little kids
They are gone
For the four years
Each Christmas one disappears
I can't figure out where they might go
I have cleaned every closet
And cleaned every bed
There like your brain after a stroke
It puts it in a hidden box
And it may never ever come out —

74 Somebody's angry
2/26/2020

I don't know what I did
The question I have something to do
And the angry response
Tells me being selfish

Asking you God
To help me figure it out
To help me not be that way
I didn't want to make some one angry —

75   I want to pray
3/12/2020

    Have a stroke
    So I am different now
    I rely on many things for other people
    But I'm OK to be alone at home by myself
    How or can I get out to doing some things on my own?
    I feel like I'm whining

    And now since I've had my stroke many people seem to have gone away. Friends kids grandkids everyone. Is just not there anymore and I don't know how to tell everybody I just feel alone all the time.

    And how do I figure out now with God who I am and what kind of life I am living since I'm here. I have this new life God has given me but I don't know what to do with it because I can't drive so everything revolves around other people who work all the time and it is said that it's not safe for me to use City buses and things for other people to drive me that I don't know. And I can't figure out what my life is now anyway. Whiny yes it seems that way but I don't know what else to say.

76 Retire
8/25/21

What do you do when you're going to retire?
What things do you think of to go see?
Or do you do a lot of gardening?
Or maybe are you going to go overseas?
Maybe you like to travel to go up high in the mountains?
Or maybe you want to visit family and spend a lot of time there?
Or maybe you're write a book?
Or maybe go back to school?

Or maybe you've had a stroke
And now you have Aphasia
So your numbers and words don't work
And maybe you can't drive anymore
And you might get lost on your own
So there's not much you can do on your own
It requires someone else to help you get anything done
So then what are you going to do when you retire? —

77 Routine - change

I get up in the morning
Help my husband get ready for work
I take my medicine with my boost
I read my Bible and my study

Then I make up what I'm gonna do
To do for the rest of the day
Taking care of my Ashra
I'm taking care of the house

Then I have 10 birds to take care of
Sometimes they're hard to take care of
Get them food and water
And clean up their cages

I also have 17 sugar gliders to take care of
And they are interesting to do
They get special food and get them plenty of water
I clean their cages but it's hard

It takes me all day to do what I'm gonna do
So then when I get another thing to add
Turn my routine upside down
And I had to figure out how to fit it in

I have my routine and it was all right
So how do I fit this more than one in
Three days it has been all out of whack
And I have to get it back together again —

78   Where did the Joy go?
12/20/21

When I was a kid
I love Christmas!
I love the happiness
Everyone had it!
Everyone said Merry Christmas!!

When I was A mom
I love Christmas!
Buying gifts meant so much!
And to watch others open them
Meant the world to me!

Now I have Aphasia
I still love Christmas!
But now The world isn't happy
I picked the wrong things
And the JOY just doesn't show.

Where did the Joy go?
What changed in the world?
When did it became "me first"?
Back when we enjoyed everyone!
I still love Christmas, it's Jesus! —

79   Brain is spinning!

I can't believe I said that!
I'm so angry I said that!
That's not even what I wanted to say!
And I said it to EVERYONE in church!
And I'm sad that the words hurt Jesus.
And I can't even feel like I can talk right now!!
I'm just so angry and so upset and so frustrated. —

80   I am a new person!!

I am a new person!!
The problem is the world don't let it change —

81 September 22, 2022

I am babysitting today.
I child I care for at church.
I really want to do this so much!
I thought as a mom and kids,
I should be able to do this.

I do have Aphasia. —

82 Where do you belong

Where do you belong in this world?
When I'm done here on this world I'm going to heaven with God.

But I cannot find my world here yet —

83   I believe we need to love others.
5/16/22

Living on a desert island by yourself.
No other people around you. Kind of silly yes but we think about it often.
But in the morning when it's time to get up what makes you feel good to get up?

Then you have to go get food and water, take a bath, wash your clothes and clean up your little place… then what do you do?

16 or more hours in a day, talking to yourself will get boring after a while.

Reading the same books you can probably just say the words eventually.

No one to take care of and no one to take care of you. No one to tell you they love you or that you love them. Not even anyone to help you clean up the mess!

Without one person, what's the point? To be alone every day Is to die. —

84 How do you decide?
4/21/21

The spouse-
Oh my God my loved one had a stroke!
They're asleep I pray they wake up!
I need you to live because I love you!!
I need to take care of you and provide for you!
Then as you get better there is just so much more!
Like Chores dishes laundry taking care of my things!
It's all because I love you!

The stroke-
I never knew I was asleep. Waking up was nice.
Don't remember anything but many people care about me.
I knew everyone was important I just didn't know why.
I did everything they asked me to do actually got a little bit better.
Then it became do I do therapy or do I do other chores?
Which one is more important?
I can't do both? which one? which one?
Well I try to work on both because
I really love you and I have to take care of me! —

85   Autobiography

I had my stroke
August 20 of 2016.
My husband found me on the floor.
And I was unconscious.
And he called the ambulance about 7:00 AM.
I remember a gentleman in the ambulance
That kept calling me my name
But I couldn't answer him,
And then I was unconscious again.
The first thing I remember was being wheeled out and hearing people talk.
To me, that was Monday night.
My family tells me I was awake Sunday afternoon after church.
I couldn't talk much, I could say Trebor (I knew what it meant) and I smile all the time.
And my son made a song and I can sing that, and that made them all happy.
I was able to walk and mostly use my hands. My husband taught me how to write my name because I have to be able to do that but that's all I can do.
Then I believe on Thursday it was all done, 6 days.
And then as far as I know I left the hospital and went home.

My husband went to work each day.
My son came and stayed with me and provided great things for me.
They found me a great place for speech to help me,
Who also taught me about STAR!
So I was doing really well learning and being able to do the things I need to do.

After about a year I was able to stay home by myself.
 My Son continue take me to STAR for about two years until he got a job and then I have to do it by the bus.

I am able to make dinner and wash the dishes,
I can do the laundry and take out the trash,
I can vacuum and dust and mop,
I take care of the animals and pay my own bills,
So, for the most part,
I think I'm doing fairly well and taking care of myself. And I do pretty good about making my own mess and trying to clean it up.

now I'm trying to find my way, if that makes any sense.
Things that keep me busy that I enjoy;
Painting, crochet, gardening (I love flowers), poetry, books,
Drawing, A lot of things I might try! Oh and people! I love to watch people! —

86 Special
7/28/22

How do you become something special?
Will you try something to be kind for everyone,
And loving and caring to each one,
And doing the jobs the best you can,
And it still doesn't seem to be enough.
I see other people make special dinners,
Or cycling all over the place,
Or writing books to help other people,
Or caring for other families,
How can can they do it?
Everyone tells them how wonderful and special they are.
And me I just give up because nothing I do is special it's just here. —

87   21

Get out!
Move out!
Watch your mouth.
Many people are angery.
You don't Open the window to say goodbye
I think you've been different for a while Married but not.
It's sad because I will love you forever regardless.
Dear Heavenly Father,
Help me to go to Heaven with you. I don't want to hurt people anymore. It was wrong for him to say it with out God.

Can you be dead without dying? —

88   Strokeaversary
8/20/22

6 years ago today,
My Stokeaversary.
I almost died.
Today, I wish I had. —

89   My Dad
5/4/22

Go to see my dad.
He had a stroke in March 2016.
I mean it was so scary.
He was only in the hospital one day!
And everything else was OK.
He went to occupational therapy,
But he didn't like that so he didn't no more.
He's done very good with everything at that point
I still has friends that he's visiting
Which was wonderful!
Then sometime around 2017,
He fell from one of his heart medicines
And he had another stroke!
And this one was a little bit rougher.
His words are rough sometimes,
He has a hard time writing.
Noise like TVs and radios
It's just too much!

Dad has had two strokes.

How do you know when people tell you you're important?

I mean what tells You that They are?

What does your husband say that tells you every day how much they love you?
Do they show it to you or do they tell it to you or somehow do you just No?

Do your kids or your grandkids say they love you how do they tell you that? With Gifts or cards or
Do they just say it?

So how do you know?

Bad words!! In Church!! LaDonna!! Wow!! —

90   "Aphasia, loss of language NOT intellect" 4/27/22

Life is different now.
I am disabled.
I had a stroke,
And I have aphasia.
"Aphasia, loss of language NOT intellect".
I'm married and raised four kids.
I went to college later in life, then had a job for almost 20 years.
But now I'm not good with numbers, nor with words.
Driving by myself is not an option, I use a bus to get around.
So a job is out of the question.
I love going to church to spend time with my church family!
I have caregivers that help me often times.
But I really enjoy helping other people.
Getting things done that are very helpful.
And they remind me how GOOD Jesus is.
But I'm not able to help other people much, I guess it's because of my disability.
I can't help them with money because mine pays all my bills.
So it's hard to figure out where you are in life, just living day by day.
When wondering where to be in five years, it will still all be the same.
"Aphasia, loss of intelligence not intellect"; but wondering for me WHAT will make a difference? —

91 Personal effects
4/26/22

Mostly happy
Love to smile
Babies, giggle
Pets, hug
Kids, Bearhug
People, Helping
Me, Loving
Brain, disabled
Changes, Life
People, choices
Taken, thoughts
Never, same
me, different —

92 1,000,000 miles an hour

I am so tired
I want to sleep
I take my medicine
And wait until 10.

Get my " business" done
Tell my birds good night
Call the dogs "in the bed"
And I turn off the lights.

I close my eyes
And a picture start
Running through my eye balls
Just as fast as they can! —

93   **Momma**
2/11/2023

My granddaughter, Stasia
Take me to Clovis yesterday
To see my mom
And to take her flowers.
That was very helpful.
And then I got to tell my mother again
How much I miss her,
And I'm sorry I wasn't very nice to her.
It was nice to do
And I enjoyed it.
And I thank you Jesus for listening to me. —

94   Angry
2/8/23

There are many things
I just don't seem to understand.
Like why I am angry
 all the time!
I think about my mama,
And I wasn't very nice to her.
And she passed away,
And I was never able to say I'm sorry.
Yell at the dog,
Even yelling bad words!
My spouse, I just don't understand.
I know he's sick,
And his body really hurts!
So why do I get angry
That he can help me?
My kids are my grandkids
Hearts are hurting,
And I get very angry
 that I can't fix it!
And then I get angry at myself.
I have so many chores to do,
Because I have to do them by myself,
When do I get to do my stuff?

My therapy, my writing, my poems, my life.
I know that God has given me a purpose,
I just don't know yet what purpose is.
And sometimes it scares me,
Because I'm still sick.
I don't know how to get rid of the anger.
And I don't want to hurt anyone in the process.
But I'm hurting myself.
So, what can I do? —

95 Sandra Hash
2/17/23

Sandra, I met you 6 1/2 years ago at STAR.
You were always so kind to me, and you could laugh and giggle!
Since I had had my stroke, I really didn't feel like I had friends.
But when I met you, you always told me "friend friend"!
And I told you friend back!
We went to camp, and we loved painting and music!
And I just enjoyed the time spent with you with everything you had been through, and you almost always smile!

I used to get tickled when you said "coffee, coffee", Sandra needs coffee!

And then there were many times when she would get to Star as fast as she could, so she could tell me she got a new purse!!! She loved new purses!

And she was just a beautiful young lady every day. And I know she is with Jesus now.

She can talk and laugh and run and smile, and I am thankful for that.

But I am going to miss her. She was my friend and she won't be able to call me anymore and say "hi hi", just to brighten my day.

I love you, Sandra, and I thank you for being my friend and I will see you when you come to my time with Jesus again.

96   Untitled

You wake up
Take the dogs out to pee
You make it to pee first
But don't count on it.
You get some want something to drink,
Anything else I might need before they leave.
Then you say bye
And start your day.
You might put on some other clothes
Then you might not.
The beds need to be made
Or maybe not.
The toilets need to be cleaned
They always do,
Pee, pee everywhere you know.
Sinks and showers ain't no fun.
Dusting is everywhere,

We live in Texas,
It's dust city.
Clean the dishes,
It's always dirty.
And cleaning the dishwasher to.
Then laundry out the Wazoo!
That is constant,
And I hate it.
Somewhere in here, the dogs have to go potty again
And again, and again.
And in here somewhere, we need to vacuum the house
And mop everything.
Now it's time to eat!
And the dishes are dirty again! —

97   Untitled

An adult tells a child. You cannot tell this, this is a secret.
A teenager takes a child to a dangerous place. They say you can't tell anyone. This is a secret.
A man or a woman has carried them behind a tree and raped them, but you can't tell anyone this is a secret.
Kids in high school doing drugs in the bathroom, but his kids can't tell anyone that's a secret.
A grandparent fighting, scratching, and yelling but you can't tell anyone because it's a secret.

How has it become "right" to keep a secret that is wrong?
When did it become "OK" with a sin and not telling others they are wrong?
The silent treatment, yelling, fighting, always thinking you're right, any of those things when you're wrong means you are still wrong!

Child abuse
Beating up your loved ones
Drugs
Alcohol
Guns
Fighting
Yelling
And so many more…
It's been around for years and years
But it's still wrong, and we should not allow it to happen to anyone.

ABOUT THE AUTHOR

LaDonna Akens Elam, 64, lives in Lubbock, TX. She is married with 4 grown children. She has thirty grandchildren and 4 great-grandchildren. She worked as a Case Administrator for Robert B. Wilson for twenty years before she had her stroke in August of 2016. She was diagnosed with aphasia. Aphasia is an impairment of language, affecting the production or comprehension of speech and the ability to read or write. She continues to have difficulty with numbers and words. She records her words and uses poetry to continue moving forward.

Words Lost in the Brain is LaDonna putting her life back together with her words.

www.ingramcontent.com/pod-product-compliance
Lightning Source LLC
Chambersburg PA
CBHW071706040426
42446CB00011B/1938